"Great relationships do not just happen; they take work, priority and focus. This book gives a road map with 52 stops along the way. Engaged couples, read this book before you begin your new adventure together. Couples who have some miles on, read this book to make the adjustments to journey towards a great relationship. *Love that Lasts* is a toolkit of practical tips to enable you as a couple to move through the transitions of life successfully."

Dr. Bruce Gordon
DIRECTOR, MENTOR MATRIX SERVICES INC.

"Sometimes in life we find ourselves with more questions than answers. With the passage of time we began to understand that it's not about having all the answers but about the journey. Then answers come in the journey. This inspiring book leads you on a step by step journey of discovery that may take you to some new places and provide some new foundational anchors for life and relationships."

Nathan Hildebrandt
EXECUTIVE DIRECTOR, LEADERIMPACT GROUP

"We have read a lot of books for couples and this is one of our favorites. The content is brief, relevant, helpful and best of all effectively moves couples to meaningful conversation. Read the book. But even more importantly, use it to have the quality conversations you need."

Neil and Sharol Josephson
NATIONAL DIRECTORS, FAMILYLIFE CANADA

LOVE
THAT LASTS

52 Insights for Couples

Mike Woodard

FAMILYLIFE | POWER to Change

Love That Lasts: 52 Insights for Couples

by Mike Woodard

ISBN 978-1-894605-95-3

Power to Change Ministries
20385 64 Avenue, Langley, BC V2Y 1N5 Canada

info@powertochange.org
familylifecanada.com / powertochange.com

Cover, design and production by Bill Glasgow, Abbotsford (604-853-8666)

Cover images © Getty Images/Hemera/Thinkstock

Printed in Canada

Contents

Mike and Karen Woodard with their two grandsons, Domonic and Coby.

E veryone yearns for a relationship that is deep, rich and satisfying! We desire companionship that brings comfort, contentment, and passion that will survive the storms of life.

This collection of relationship insights is intended to stimulate discussion, explore practical steps in your relationship and most of all, to keep you talking! Relational growth is proportional to our level of consistent soul connection. In the avalanche of life's demands, it's easy to lose our grip on the most important relationship we have with our spouse.

You may have noticed the sub title, *52 Insights for Couples*. The genesis of this collection has come from a weekly relationship tip posted on the FamilyLife Canada web site. The intent of having a "weekly" tip is to allow time for talking, reflecting and taking practical steps of application. Think of these 52 relationship insights like vitamins. You take them regularly for greatest benefit. Take them all at once and you could do harm, so you should instead digest them one at a time.

If you picture for a moment just where your relationship could be a year from now, if you developed a weekly habit of thoughtful dialogue, what would that look like? Strength, depth and richness in a love relationship are built by intentional regular investments of focus and time, so let's get started!

Appreciation is received by the soul like rain after a drought! It is so life giving. Appreciation is also a significant motivator. Much in life is taken for granted. A simple thank you or acknowledgement goes a long way to encourage a weary heart. What do you appreciate about the people around you? Tell them.

ACTION Think of 3 things you have taken for granted today and say thank you. It can be really simple. Some examples…

- Thanks for dinner. What a great meal!
- Thanks for filling the car with gas. I appreciate it.
- Thanks for doing the wash. This shirt smells so good.
- Wow, the kitchen looks so clean. I sure like the way you take care of things.
- You do an amazing job with the yard, thank you.
- You look good. I appreciate the way you take care of yourself.
- You are so patient. I sure appreciate it.

You get the idea…

Proverb of Solomon:

"The right word at the right time is like precious gold set in silver."

– Proverbs 25:11 CEV

Conflict Management

Conflict is a normal part of any relationship! Conflict can be constructive or destructive depending on how it is managed.

In the book *The 10 Best Decisions a Couple Can Make*, Bill and Pam Farrel state that research shows there are many styles of effective conflict resolution. The key word is effective. They present some characteristics that flow from both.

EFFECTIVE CONFLICT

- You feel better about your relationship when you are done talking.
- You have confidence that your future disagreements will enhance your relationship.
- The process of making up is positive for both people.

INEFFECTIVE CONFLICT

- You feel worse about your relationship when you are done talking.
- You start to avoid or dread serious conversations.
- Your arguments do not lead to making up.
- You become increasingly critical of one another.

If you are getting more check marks on the ineffective list you may be headed for relationship dysfunction.

ACTION   Talk about how you feel and what ineffective conflict management is doing to your relationship. Establish some ground rules for dealing with conflict that you both agree on.

SUGGESTED RESOURCE   *The 10 Best Decisions a Couple Can Make* by Bill and Pam Farrel

I n the classic book, *His Needs, Her Needs* author Willard E. Harley Jr. suggests there are 10 common needs in relationships.

1. **Sexual Fulfillment** Sexual availability and responsiveness.
2. **Recreational Companionship** Involvement in activities that you both enjoy.
3. **Attractive Spouse** The attractiveness of your spouse makes you feel great.
4. **Domestic Support** Creation of a peaceful and well-managed home.
5. **Admiration** Desire to be respected, valued and appreciated.
6. **Affection** Thoughtful expression of care.
7. **Conversation** Characterized by information, mutual interest, dialogue and full attention.
8. **Honesty and Openness** Open conversation about thoughts, feelings, likes, dislikes, personal history, and plans for the future.
9. **Financial Support** Financial security.
10. **Family Commitment** Active in the development of the children.

Meeting the top 4 needs is essential for security in the relationship to be affair proof. If the top 4 or 5 needs are not met in the relationship the person will seek to have them met elsewhere! That's why Harley's subtitle is "Building an Affair Proof Marriage."

ACTION Pick your top five. Give the list to your spouse/partner and ask them to do the same. Talk about your list. Talk about how these needs are being met. Talk about the areas that still need some attention. Review the list in a month to track your progress as a couple.

SUGGESTED RESOURCE *His Needs, Her Needs* by Willard E. Harley Jr.

Sometimes picturing the worst case scenario can help set perspective. Picture your relationship as a staircase. If breaking up is the worst case scenario, picture that at the bottom. At the top picture the best case scenario, a relationship with great intimacy, honesty, teamwork, affection… You finish the list. Where are you on the staircase? Maybe a more important question… Which way is your relationship moving? What's taking you up toward a great relationship? What's moving you down in the wrong direction?

ACTION Take inventory of your relationship. If you continue as things are now will you have the relationship you want in the future? Be intentional about a plan to move to the next step on the staircase. What is one thing you could do to improve the quality of your relationship? Maybe it is as simple as having coffee together 2 times a week? Maybe it's putting a date night in the schedule?

EXAMPLE My wife and I found talking about our schedules for the coming week every Sunday night was a really simple step that improved communication, planning and helped us understand the demands we each faced in the coming week. This simple habit has produced many benefits.

Did you know…

"In Canada, 4 in 10 first time marriages end in divorce."

– CBC Report: October 4, 2010

Listening is foundational to good communication. All marriage specialists agree on that point. Stephen Covey states this principle in his book, *The 7 Habits of Highly Effective People;* "Seek first to understand, then to be understood."

The Bible also has wisdom on this: "Be quick to hear, slow to speak and slow to anger," James 1:19.

Here are some tips:

Check your understanding. You might want to say, "Can I repeat what I think you just said to be sure I understand correctly?"

MEN   **Do not seek to fix things** unless you have permission.
You could ask, "Do you want me to simply listen or are you looking for a solution?"

WOMEN   Feeling and emotions are good. Realize **it might be hard for your guy to understand the main point if you are emotional,** so clarify the main point for him.
You might want to say, "I know I'm really emotional but this ____ is important to me."

MEN   **She may not believe you understand unless you identify with her emotions.**
Say something like, "I hear your frustration… anger… hurt…."

SUGGESTED RESOURCE   *The 7 Habits of Highly Effective People* by Stephen Covey

Not an Australian creation but a new perspective: what you give is what you get. **The best sex is a GIVING experience.** The principle is this: If you commit to giving pleasure, the natural outcome is that you will receive pleasure in return. Just like a boomerang it will come back to you. It may take time, patience and discipline depending on the history of the relationship. The reward will be worth the investment. Make it your goal to give the greatest sexual satisfaction to your partner. You will have the joy in knowing that you provide a kind of pleasure that can only be found in your physical relationship together!

The ability to make sex a giving experience comes from two character qualities; discipline and selflessness. Both are rooted in a willingness to place your own desires behind the needs or desires of your partner. In a world that seems to be shaped by instant gratification and selfishness these qualities are on the endangered list. Pornography and self gratification are destructive to sexual satisfaction because they promote instant gratification and selfish indulgence of sexual desires.

ACTION Make a commitment to give pleasure rather than focus on yourself. Be intentional in seeking ways to understand and satisfy the sexual desire of your partner. See what happens…. The ultimate goal is mutual fulfillment and satisfaction.

Are YOU having an affair? You say, "Never!" but there may be more to think about... How do you define the word "affair"? Generally we think of an affair involving another person. However, affairs come in different shapes and sizes... an affair of the mind... an affair with work, with sports, with hobbies, volunteering; the list goes on. **Anything that takes your attention, emotional energy and affection away from your primary relationship could be classed as an affair**. Have you crossed the line? So let me ask again... Are you having an affair?

ACTION Do a heart exam. Are you prioritizing your relationship? **Is your partner getting the best of your affection and attention** or is it going elsewhere? How would they answer this question?
Ask them...

NOTE This is not meant to diminish the emotional pain of a physical affair. We recognize that to be in a different category.

SUGGESTED RESOURCE *Close Calls* by Dave Carder

Baggage

© MZACH/MORGUEFILE.COM

All people come into a relationship with baggage, both physical and emotional. The physical is represented by the wedding gifts and other possessions used to put your new home together.

The other kind of baggage, emotional baggage, is less visible and often has to do with our family of origin. This baggage needs to be unpacked and sorted also. In the book *The 10 Best Decisions a Couple Can Make*, Bill and Pam Farrel suggest a couple should ask two deliberate questions:

1. **"What did our parents do that we want to continue doing and pass to future generations?"**
2. **"What are the things we do not want to repeat in our lives?"**

This discussion could reveal some very good things you've experienced or could touch some very difficult and painful hurts. The dialogue could help you identify and address issues in a very significant foundational way. This discussion should be an ongoing one throughout your relationship; it is never too late to start. It will be like peeling an onion, one layer at a time.

ACTION **Step One:** Pick a private place and ask the questions. You might want to write down your answers. The answers might fall in three categories: Good, Bad and Ugly. Celebrate the Good. Identify the Bad. Capture the Ugly.

Step Two: Share your answers. Record your new family values. You may realize how fortunate you are. You may also uncover some deeply hurtful issues/ events that may need processing and perspective from a close friend or with professional help.

SUGGESTED RESOURCE *The 10 Best Decisions a Couple Can Make* by Bill and Pam Farrel

Many authors talk about something akin to an emotional bank account. None have made it more popular than Stephen Covey in the classic book *The Seven Habits of Highly Effective People*. The concept is that our actions toward others will make deposits or withdrawals from an emotional/relational account. Deposits are made through actions that communicate kindness, consideration, appreciation and respect. A healthy balance does allow for withdrawals. Emotional withdrawals happen when a person is inconsiderate, hurtful, impatient or insulting.

As with a personal bank account a large balance builds security and a low balance creates concern, while a deficit is stressful. Continued overdrafts can lead to bankruptcy. The same is true emotionally. We all make withdrawals, intentional or unintentional. Good relationships require a positive cash flow. Emotional overdraft can lead to account closure!

ACTION   Reflect on the emotional balance in your relationship? What are ways you can make a deposit this week? On a regular basis?

EXAMPLE   My wife makes deposits whenever she expresses appreciation. Each time she says, "Thank you, I appreciate…" a deposit is made in my account on her behalf. I make a major deposit when I clean the bathroom, mop the kitchen floor or vacuum. All things I know she does not like to do.

SUGGESTED RESOURCE   *The Seven Habits of Highly Effective People* by Stephen Covey.

E veryone wants the ideal: home, car, kids, friends, everything! What about finding the ideal relationship?

There is danger in attempting to FIND the ideal; it results in unrealistic expectations! Our culture suggests we should find the perfect soul mate, but the reality is that person does not exist! No one will realistically meet all the expectations of your perfect soul mate. This common myth sets people up for major disappointment.

A better approach is to find someone with whom you want to spend the rest of your life and then work together to create a great relationship with that person, becoming true soul mates over time. It takes work and it might take a life time but the process will be worth the effort.

ACTION Accept the imperfections in your partner. Have fun holding hands on the journey of life creating your relationship through the shared joys and sorrows, successes and failures of your life together.

An increasing factor in marriage breakdown is over commitment. A fast-paced life can produce constant physical and emotional exhaustion. Relationship experts cite over commitment as one of the top five relationship killers.

How are you doing? Healthy relationships require time and attention. How often do you sit, talk or just hang out with no urgent demands? It takes self discipline not to get swept along in the hurried life. Who sets your agenda, you or someone else? Are the expectations realistic?

Symptoms of over commitment and exhaustion are hard on your relationship, and they include:

- Headaches
- Sleeplessness
- Irritability
- Emotional outbursts
- Loss of motivation

Relationships take energy! If you give your energy to everything else first, your relationship will suffer and may not survive.

ACTION Be intentional; take a serious look at your schedule and make deliberate decisions. Pace, energy and capacity are unique to the individual, so do not to compare yourself to others. Are YOU going to survive or thrive if you keep going at this pace? Don't be fooled by the myth, "It's just for a little while longer and then things will slow down."

Back in my single days a friend told me she loved me. I was surprised. It was awkward. I did not know what to say because I did not love her in the same way. She was a dear friend but I was not "in love" with her. I will never forget her response. She said, "I love you and it is a gift. I expect nothing from you." Wow, that was profound. The unconditional nature of that statement set me free in the relationship; we continued as close friends.

Unconditional love is hard to find, yet unforgettable when you do find it! It is a gift freely given and provides deep security in a relationship. Unconditional love is characterized by a willingness to GIVE unselfishly. This type of love comes from the character of the giver. Conditional love is based on something external. It has strings attached and sounds like, "I will love you if you are strong or successful or beautiful." There are conditions attached, which create fear and insecurity in a relationship.

ACTION Does your love have strings attached? Will you consider giving the gift of unconditional love?

Reflect on this description of love…

> " Love is patient, love is kind. It does not envy, it does not boast, it is not proud. It does not dishonor others, it is not self-seeking, it is not easily angered, it keeps no record of wrongs. Love does not delight in evil but rejoices with the truth. It always protects, always trusts, always hopes, always perseveres."
>
> *- St. Paul's Letter to the Corinthians (I Cor. 13:4-7)*

SUGGESTED RESOURCE See "Karen's Story" on page *a-4* at the end of the book

W hen our children were little they would often protest, "That's not fair!" I'm sure I said it when I was a kid. My kind and gentle parental response was… "Life is not fair. In fact you would not like it if it was totally fair."

An adult version of the same thought is "50/50 relationships." My response is still the same. "Relationships are not 50/50. You would not like it even if it was 50/50." Having a 50/50 mindset is not productive because it does not work for at least 5 reasons:

1. **It's too hard to keep track.** Monitoring the 50/50 takes too much work.
2. **It creates a "you owe me" dynamic.** That sucks the fun out of life and leads to anger.
3. **It does not factor in skills, strengths, energy levels and passions.** I'm better at some things, my wife at others and we have very different energy levels and motivations.
4. **It does not factor in "seasons of life."** Demands of family, work and education are ever changing. Going the extra distance is needed for survival.
5. **It's Bad Relationship Math.** Do you really want to give half, 50% to your relationship? 100/100 is better math.

ACTION Commit to being all in. Do what it takes. Stop keeping score!

"Do nothing out of selfish ambition or vain conceit. Rather, in humility value others above yourselves, not looking to your own interests but each of you to the interests of the others."

- St. Paul in a letter to the Philippians (Philippians 2:3-4)

I could not believe my eyes; a toddler riding a tricycle on a busy street! Pulling my car over as quickly as I could, I guided the little guy off the street to the sidewalk. I did not see an adult anywhere. I asked his name and where he lived, but it was clear he could not tell me. I did not want to leave him alone, so I walked with him until his frantic parents found us and he was safely reunited with his family. I shudder to think what could have happened….

Toddlers are not intended to face the dangers of life alone. As humbling as it may sound we are all like this toddler, not meant to go through life on our own. Relationships are riddled with challenges, difficulties and even dangers, and just as I guided this innocent traveler to safety, God desires to walk beside us through this life. Your relationship with your partner will look a lot different when each of you are allowing God to work in such a way that you are experiencing His unconditional love, forgiveness, joy, patience, kindness and self control.

ACTION Have you wandered off on your own spiritually? Are you going through life without God's presence and resources? Ask Him to walk beside you as you navigate traffic and all of the challenges of living in our fast-paced world.

SUGGESTED RESOURCE See Appendices in the back of this book

Have you ever heard the statement, "Attitude is everything!"?

In the book *Creating an Intimate Marriage*, Jim Burns suggests five attitude adjustments that create a more positive and satisfying relationship:

1. **Stop Complaining.** Criticism shuts down intimacy. No one wants to be naked with someone who is critical!
2. **Show Gratitude.** It is amazing what a simple "thank you" will do in a relationship.
3. **Practice the Golden Rule.** "Do to others what you would have them do to you." –Jesus. However, many couples today adhere to the rule that says: "Do to others what they do to you." This is a "tit-for-tat" mentality that only contributes to resentment and spite.
4. **Control the "If Only's..."** "If only my spouse would do this, I would be happy": Happiness is internal. No external action or person can fill another's void or desire for happiness.
5. **Choose Fun and Optimism.** Be intentional. Think of one fun thing to add to your marriage. What did you do for fun when you were dating?

ACTION Review the list. Pick only one area to work on and start to apply it to your relationship today.

SUGGESTED RESOURCE *Creating an Intimate Marriage* by Jim Burns

You Need to Change!

Be honest, when you read the title, who did you think of? Was it the person you wake up next to each morning? Have you ever read a book or article and thought of many applications… for the people around you? I do it all the time.

Gandhi said,

"Be the change you wish to see in the world."

I challenge you to be the change you wish to see in your relationship. What would that look like?

- If you want to have more fun, be more fun.
- If you want more communication, ask questions and learn to listen well.
- If you want more sex, be more loving.
- If you want more appreciation, start saying thank you more often.

At best you are the only one you can change… so start with that.

ACTION Think about the changes you would like to see in your relationships and start with yourself.

D oes boredom kill relationships? Yes, it can! While routine might bring order and stability to life, it is true that it can also engender boredom. So, here are four rut-busters that can add some spice and creativity to your marriage relationship.

■ **Buy a small gift on a "No Special Occasion" day.** It's not a birthday, anniversary or Valentine's Day gift. Surprise your partner and say: "I was thinking about you today and got you a little something…"

■ **Write a note and leave it out for your unsuspecting spouse to read and cherish.** Say some of those things you should say more often like "I love you, I appreciate you…"

■ **Do something you never do!** Cook a meal, clean the bathrooms, buy tickets to an event or concert they'd like, have a surprise date, or even give a massage.

■ **Spice up Sex!** Get on some crazy underwear, go to bed naked, have sex on the living room floor, use body oil, or add some candles to the bedroom… Use your imagination!

ACTION Pick one thing on this list and do it this week. Remember to pick something that is "unpredictable" and unforgettable! Create a memorable moment.

An expert in time management was speaking to a group of business students. He pulled out a one-gallon, wide-mouth jar. Then he produced about a dozen fist-sized rocks and carefully placed them, one by one, into the jar. He asked the students, "Is this jar full?" Everyone said, "Yes."

"Really?" he replied, as he brought out a bucket of gravel. He dumped some gravel in and shook the jar. Then he asked the group once more, "Is this jar full?"

"Probably not," one of them answered. He brought out a bucket of sand and started dumping the sand in the jar. Once more he asked the question. "Is this jar full?" "No!" the class chanted, getting into the process. To conclude, he grabbed a pitcher of water and began to pour it in until the jar was filled to the brim. Then the expert asked, "What is the point of this illustration?"

One eager student offered a life application, saying, "The point is, no matter how full your schedule is, if you try really hard you can always fit some more things into it."

"No," the expert retorted, "the truth is this: If you don't put the big rocks in first, you'll never get them in."

ACTION What are the big rocks in your life? List them.

EVALUATE Has the small stuff filled the spaces needed for the really important relationship space?

DECIDE What is one thing you will do this week to prioritize the people who are important to you?

G ood communication is vital to healthy growing relationships. Defensiveness can stunt or destroy communication. Defensiveness is an attempt at protecting ourselves. It is sometimes rooted in either pride or insecurity: pride in not accepting our flaws and the way they affect our relationships; insecurity, in that we may feel overwhelmed by our perceived weaknesses.

The acceptance of who we are is the antidote to defensiveness. When we are defensive, we may be reacting in order to protect a false view of ourselves as perfect. People who think they are perfect are no fun to be around! If we are defensive because we are feeling insecure and overwhelmed, we need to step back, accept our weaknesses, but also affirm our strengths. In either case, we both come to the same conclusion: perfection only exists in heaven; everyone is flawed.

ACTION When tempted to be defensive, choose to be silent. Listen to what your partner is saying. Ask questions to help you really understand what is being communicated. Ask yourself if you are feeling threatened? What needs to be protected? Accept that even in the most unfounded criticism there can be some element of truth. Own the truth and discuss the way forward.

"… Do not think of yourself more highly than you ought, but rather think of yourself with sober judgment, in accordance with the faith God has distributed to each of you."

–St Paul in a letter to the Romans (Romans 12:3)

Don't Sweat the Small Stuff is the ability to know when to speak up and when to let things slide.

We all have limited energy and face more issues than we can ever resolve. Don't sweat the small stuff is really a reminder to invest your limited energy where it will do the most good.

Some questions that might help you figure out whether or not to invest yourself in a particular issue are:

- On a scale of 1-10, how important is this issue in the grand scheme of things?
- What would be the worst thing that would happen if this issue is not addressed?
- Is there a simple solution?

For example: I value clean counter tops more than my wife does. I could keep reminding her of the "supreme" value of clean counters. However, so far, it has not worked. I have not found that to be energy well invested.

So let's think about this… On a scale of 1-10 how important is this? Maybe a 3 compared to other things. What is the worst thing that could happen if the counters are not cleaned off? I will be irritated by crumbs on the counter. Is there a simple solution? When I notice, I wipe off counters.

ACTION List all the areas which continually create conflict between you. Together, rate them on a scale of 1-10 as to how serious they are. Decide not to sweat the small stuff.

My mother would often say, "If we were the same, one of us would not be necessary." Two people who are different have the wonderful potential of complementing each other but also having some level of conflict. Conflict is normal and can be very productive. Couples miss out on the benefits of conflict by either being too passive or being too aggressive. A common pattern of conflict mismanagement is to either withdraw or attack. Learn to engage in a positive way. You engage when you trust the other person and depth of the relationship to handle the conflict. So go have a "good" fight!

EVALUATE AS A COUPLE Do you withdraw or become aggressive?

EXPLORE What would it look like if you were to engage in conflict in a positive way?

DECIDE TOGETHER When you see the conflict cloud gathering decide to neither run nor get aggressive. ASK "What's a win/win solution for this issue?"

REMEMBER Constructive conflict is solution focused and not person focused and can build depth into any relationship.

"The mind of the wise makes their speech insightful and enhances the teaching of their lips. Pleasant words are flowing honey, sweet to the taste and healing to the bones."

– Proverb of Solomon (Proverbs 16: 23-24 CEB)

Talk! The number one thing you can do to improve your sexual life is to talk about it. Many couples find it awkward to discuss their physical relationship. Even so, it's important to take a deep breath and plunge into talking about this important topic.

Talk Before... Read an article or book together to help open the conversation and stimulate the discussion. Talk about what you enjoy about your physical relationship. Talk about what you desire or your expectations. Talk about timing, positions and frequency. Talk about foreplay, and explore what will set the mood for your partner.

Talk During... Express personal excitement and passion during sex. Tell your partner what feels good. Express appreciation. Give a "progress report" of how close you are to a climax, and direct your partner's movement and touch. Verbal expression can heighten excitement and pleasure.

Talk After... Compliment, encourage and talk about what you enjoyed.

Never talk about intimate details of your physical relationship with anyone else unless it is in a counseling context. Hold the sexual experience of your relationship as a private and delightful knowledge that bonds the two of you together!

ACTION Plan a date in a romantic atmosphere where you can begin to talk about this important topic. Which of the above suggestions do you want to start incorporating into your life together?

SUGGESTED RESOURCE *The Gift of Sex* by Clifford and Joyce Penner

The cycle goes something like this: a problem surfaces in your relationship, and one of you says, "We have a problem…" but the other person does not take it seriously so the problem is not really addressed. This happens again, then again and again! Despair takes over. One day the one that has been saying, "I need help" gives up and says, "We're done!" or leaves a note that says, "I'm gone!" This finally gets the other person's attention, but it may be too late.

"What will it take to get your attention?" In the book *The Meaning of Marriage*, authors Tim and Kathy Keller relate how Kathy got Tim's attention by lining up some of her good china, and as soon as Tim walked in the door, breaking it with a hammer. She got his attention! Some other less dramatic ways could be to say…

- I'm starting to feel so discouraged, that unless we address this issue, I don't think I can continue like this.
- I feel really alone. I don't want to go on like this.
- I have this feeling that we are drifting apart. I do not want to live this way.

ACTION Discuss together:

Are there unaddressed issues that could sink our relationship?

Are there unhelpful habits we have developed in our relationship by ignoring or not listening to each other?

What is the best way to get our attention focused on an issue that is crucial to me?

SUGGESTED RESOURCE *The Meaning of Marriage* by Tim and Kathy Keller

L ife has a way of getting far too serious. Relationships also can become too mundane or scheduled! Some of you may be saying, "Please, let life be a little less crazy!" Even so, this might be for you! Do something crazy this week. Here is a list of things to consider…

- Bring home flowers for no reason.
- Buy some crazy boxer shorts. Give them to your man.
- Serve dessert first.
- Run in the house, grab your woman, and kiss her like she has never been kissed before.
- Do three things on the "Honey Do" list without being asked!
- Make love in the kitchen.
- Cook up a candle light dinner on Wednesday instead of waiting for a special occasion.
- Leave notes all over the house with reasons you love and appreciate the other person.
- Just sit and talk for an hour. Don't do anything, just talk.
- Buy massage oil and give each other a massage.
- Watch 5 funny YouTube videos together.
- Take turns making faces. Take pictures of the funniest ones and put them on Facebook.
- Put on loud music, dance and sing.
- Have a pudding fight.

ACTION Do something crazy!

25

A couple celebrating 60 years of marriage was asked the secret of their success. "Simple," the husband responded, "We decided early on in our relationship, I would make the big decisions. And the wife would make the small decisions. That was the last big decision we had to make!"

Humor aside, some people spend a lot of time agonizing over decisions. This stress could be tempered by learning to distinguish between trivial and important decisions. Prioritizing focus on the important allows one's limited emotional energy to be invested where it is most needed.

If every decision is difficult perhaps a person is taking themselves and life too seriously. Or perhaps it is really a matter of seeking to over control situations. *Control* demands involvement in everything and every decision. Having to control everyone and everything is exhausting. First of all, it is an impossible expectation. Secondly, seeking control drains the life blood out of relationships! Relationships thrive in an environment of trust, respect and freedom.

ACTION   Evaluate how decisions are made in your relationship. Are you satisfied with the decision making process? Are there areas where there is a desire for greater trust, respect and freedom?

26

I remember having a fleeting thought on my honeymoon, "Maybe I married the wrong person." Later my bride put that same thought into words!

That was over 30 years ago. You might be asking, "What preserved a marriage that had such doubts?"

We discovered that even in the best marriages, everyone has doubts sooner or later. Doubts are normal. They come as we discover things about our relationship or the other person that we did not know. These surprises make us question our relationship. But what we do with the doubts is absolutely crucial. We decided that each doubt, problem or conflict would be a building block, not a stumbling stone in our relationship. We also determined we would always work through the issues. It has not been easy, and I cannot say that there have not been moments of despair but each time we made it through another problem it added strength, character and resiliency to our relationship.

ACTION Make the commitment:

Resolve together that you will commit to working through your doubts, problems and conflicts, not allowing them to be stumbling stones in your relationship. Affirm your commitment to each other.

27

Every relationship has some level of disappointment, hurt and unmet expectations. No relationship will survive without forgiveness. I can attest to this personally. I had a really poor relationship with my father, who was an alcoholic. When he drank he became either a "sad drunk" or a "mad drunk". My mother ended up in the hospital because of the violence in our home.

Our relationship got worse each day until someone, whom I had wronged significantly, forgave me. Not only did they forgive me, but they started treating me like a family member. All of a sudden I began to understand forgiveness and love. If someone could treat me like that, how could I not do the same with my Dad? That example of forgiveness and love transformed my relationship with my father and has shaped all my relationships since. While all of the memories remained, the pain began to fade.

That someone was God. It was such a relief to experience God's love and forgiveness! Because He changed my life so drastically, I want to be like Him. As a result, I have come to see God's forgiveness of me as an example of the way I want to relate to others.

CONSIDER   Do you find it hard to forgive others?

REFLECT   Have you ever experienced forgiveness? What was it like?

PROMISE   God provides the ultimate love and forgiveness. Experiencing God's love and forgiveness will drastically change your life and relationships.

SUGGESTED RESOURCE   See "Mike's Story" on page *a-2* at the end of the book

28

S o often I hear the words, "How did we get here?" from couples who are wondering how they have ended up feeling miles apart. We all change and grow. Couples that grow together do some simple things to ensure they keep their friendship growing.

They spend regular time together. Whether it's a daily 15 minutes to check in with each other or a weekly evening together, they are intentional about spending time on their relationship together. (Sunday night after the kids were asleep worked well for us.) A regular date night, once a week or once a month, can also give space for time together.

They know what is happening in each other's lives. They ask questions that go deeper than exchanging facts. They keep in touch with their separate worlds of work, recreation and emotions.

They share some common interests. Books, movies, sports, home renovations, outdoor activities, video games, card games, church, or community involvement could be on the list. Couples that grow together know they must share some activities as a couple.

ACTION Set aside some couple time in your weekly schedules to connect.
Ask questions to understand the other person's world.
Develop a new interest together or resurrect an old favorite. It could be as simple as reading a book together or watching a program together that makes you laugh, think and talk.

The Change Curve?

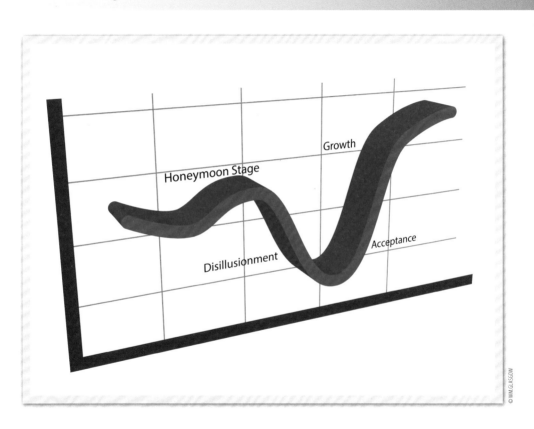

29

Did you know that every time we go through a major change we have a four stage response? The first is the **Honeymoon stage** with high emotions and excitement. The second stage is **Disillusionment.** This hits when your excitement and ideal world collide with the imperfect reality. From disillusionment you either move to **Acceptance** or **Rejection.**

Rejection means the needed change is too extreme and the work too hard. Rejection normally leads to escape, either physically or emotionally.

Acceptance leads to a Growth phase. Reality is accepted, as is the process involved in growing the relationship. Acceptance is the ingredient that leads to the wonderful maturing of a relationship, where two people choose to work together to form something that is not perfect but is still really good!

Note of Caution: A Danger of Easy Rejection is giving up too easily on building something that could be really good. A Danger of Easy Acceptance is continuing too long in an unhealthy relationship.

EVALUATE Where on the change curve are you in your relationship: honeymoon, disillusionment, acceptance or rejection? Have you already left emotionally?

CONSIDER What is the reality of your relationship? If you were to fully engage in the process of growing in this relationship, what would that look like?

COMMIT Commit yourself to accepting the reality of your relationship and the process needed for you to grow with it.

30

The recipe for a great relationship has several key ingredients. Kindness is at the top of the list for many relationships experts. Even simple acts of kindness can add such a subtle flavor so as to satisfy the hungriest of souls.

Encarta Dictionary defines kindness as: "the tendency to be sympathetic and compassionate, or an act that shows consideration and caring."

Think of ways you can sprinkle kindness into your relationships. Maybe you can write a simple thank you to someone. Maybe you can offer a helping hand. Maybe you can give a small but thoughtful gift. Coffee or chocolate always works for me. Each of these communicates value, respect and caring. Or, maybe you can offer forgiveness to someone who hurt you. Forgiveness is a wonderful gift.

ACTION Determine that you will intentionally look for ways to add kindness to your relationships.

St. Paul has some great advice…

"Be kind to one another, tender-hearted, forgiving each other, just as God in Christ also has forgiven you."

- Ephesians 4:32

31

Communication can be a challenge at the best of times. The ***LifeReady*** series, **Marriage Oneness**, offers a very helpful approach that has helped Karen and me to be more patient with each other. Host Tim Lundy discusses different communication styles:

- **Land the Plane** versus **Enjoy the Ride** communicators.

- **Share Your Feelings** versus **Just the Facts** communicators.

- **Think Out Loud** versus **Let's Take Turns** communicators.

We have found that understanding our style can help us relax, laugh and be better communicators! It's amazing how understanding the differences can help reduce stress. For example: If you are in a relationship with a "Land the Plane" person and you are an "Enjoy the Ride" person it would be good to identify that difference. It's amazing how understanding differences can help reduce stress. I tend to be a "Land the Plane" communicator, and my wife is more of an "Enjoy the Ride" conversationalist, so just knowing that makes us both more patient with each other.

ACTION Make a date with each other to meet at a favorite coffee shop.
Identify your styles of communication.
Discuss a time you have felt most frustrated and how understanding each other's style might help.

SUGGESTED RESOURCE *Marriage Oneness*/LifeReady Series

32

Agree or Disagree? The happiest people are those with low expectations.

An expectation is the mental picture of an anticipated outcome. Unrealistic expectations generally lead to disappointment. Even realistic expectations will result in disappointments from time to time. High expectations can inspire if they are managed well. In relationships, our expectations can come from a variety of helpful and not so helpful sources: the media, books, internet and experience.

Some helpful principles in shaping and managing expectations are:

- **The ideal is a phantom...reality is never perfect.** Don't be robbed of something really good by a phantom that is not achievable.
- **Disappointment is part of life and relationships.** Forgive quickly and move on with making the relationship grow. Don't let disappointments in your relationship stop you in your tracks.
- **Deal with the expectations of self first.** Figure out what you expect from yourself before you start laying blame or expectations on your partner. It may surprise you how realistic your expectations will become when you start with yourself first.

ACTION Evaluate which of these principles is true of the way you manage your expectations. In which do you need to grow?

DECIDE What is one thing you can do today to become more effective at managing your expectations?

"Do nothing out of selfish ambition or vain conceit, but in humility consider others better than yourself. Each of you should look not only to your own interests, but also to the interests of others."

- St. Paul in his letter to the Philippians 2:3-4

33

Stress can kill you! Some authors estimate anywhere from 50-70 percent of doctors' visits are stress related. The physical toll of financial stress is scary. Relationships are destroyed by the pressure of financial mismanagement. Some stress we cannot control, but financial stress is often self-inflicted.

Over spending is self indulgent and leads to stress. It can be intentional or unintentional. Unintentional is normally related to careless management. Small slippage can lead to the end of the month question, "Where did all our money go?" My wife and I wrote down every dime we spent for one month to discover the leakage. It was actually little things like the coffee, the snacks, the small indulgences that were contributing to "more month than money!"

The intentional spending may be more difficult to control. Commitment to some simple principles of money management may help. Here are three:

- **No Impulse Buying:** Wait 24 hours to purchase a big ticket item and have agreement on what limit constitutes a major purchase. (Our limit started at $50.)
- **No Interest on Credit:** Credit cards are put away the moment the total cannot be paid in full when due.
- **No Lone Ranger Action:** Without a partnership you will fail. Hold each other accountable.

ACTION Ask the following questions: On a scale of 1-10 how stressed are you feeling about finances? Which of the 3 rules are being violated? Agree on principles and steps for reducing the stress you are feeling.

34

When a relationship is born, two people come together with individual identities. These individual identities are what attracted you in the first place. The new identity is the one you form together as a couple, as you blend two lives into a life together: your shared identity.

A shared identity is BEST formed by two people who have and continue to develop healthy individual identities. This merging includes a willingness to share opinions and work towards combining traditions, values and future goals. Some values are imported from the family of origin, and others form in the new perspectives you share together. Healthy relationships combine individual interests with shared identity to express who you are as a couple.

Decisions become more complex and are no longer based solely on individual desires; they consider what is best for both the relationship and the individuals. Some authors describe this shift from "me to we". Forging a way of life together creates a unique fabric and strength in the relationship which is particularly satisfying. This shared identity takes time to form and is dynamic; it will evolve as you experience life stages together.

Unhealthy patterns can exist in one of two extremes: being overly dependent or overly independent. Both extremes will sabotage the development of a strong relationship and this shared identity.

ACTION Discuss the shared identity you currently have as a couple. Do you both like your shared identity? Discuss your individual identity; are you independent or overly dependent?

Out is not an Option!

35

E veryone can look back at moments that have shaped the rest of their lives for good or bad. Relationships also have defining moments. A huge defining moment in my marriage was when I made up my mind that **"Out is not an Option!"** I would be faithful and committed to one woman for the rest of my life. That decision has shaped the outcome of many discouraging moments when I wanted to throw in the towel, quit or just give up. My decision was made! My energy could then be directed toward working through the discouragement and doubts to strengthen the relationship.

Problems have become building blocks to our relationship. My resolution that "Out is not an Option" has caused me to be focused on solutions!

ACTION Decide today that "out is not an option". Determine that, as of today, there is no "out". Resolve to work through the difficulties focused on solutions and the future of your relationship.

36

I ran a marathon on the opening day of Expo '86 in Vancouver. Training was really difficult: I trained in the cold weather, ice and snow of Edmonton, Alberta. My training partner injured himself early into our training. My mental picture of crossing the finish line kept me going through the challenges and pain of training alone through that long winter. That picture contributed to my success and deep satisfaction on the day of the marathon.

Do you have a mental picture of "crossing the finish line"? What do you want your finish line to look like? The day I leave this planet I want to have been faithful to one amazing woman. I want to be deeply missed because I was a wonderful friend. I want to have shared rich moments that linger long in the memories of those that think of me. I want my children to admire the way I lived life and loved them. I want to enter eternity and hear the words from God, "Well done, my good and faithful servant." This picture helps me to meet the challenges of each day.

ACTION Paint the picture!

ENVISION What are the 3 or 4 things you want people to remember about you? What kinds of memories do you want to leave your family? What are the words you would like to hear from God at the end of your life?

Perspective on Sex...

37

O ur perspective on sex can be influenced by many different factors: past experiences, libido, gender, age! Consider a few statements. With which do you identify the most?

- One person may view sex as an expression of affection. The other may view sex as a result of affection.
- One person may view sex as a way to build an emotional bond. The other may view sex as an expression of an emotional bond.
- One person may view sex as a way to a healthy relationship. The other may view sex as coming from a healthy relationship.
- One person may view sex as a way of feeling close. The other may view sex as a result of feeling close.

ACTION Meet your spouse for a romantic date.

DISCUSS Which statements reflect our experience and perspective? Have any of these differences created frustration in our relationship?

SHARE What factors influence your perspective?

REFLECT How might understanding your partner's perspective help ease your frustration?

Preemptive Decision Making

© GETTY IMAGES/ISTOCKPHOTO/THINKSTOCK

38

I was in a remote area of Asia. Less than 24 hours after arriving, I received a message that my mother had passed away. I started a 46 hour return trip back alone. On the way, I met an attractive young woman who spoke English. She offered to get me from the train station in Beijing to a bus to the airport, where I would have to wait all day for a flight to North America. As we traveled to the bus station she explained she had recently broken up with her boy friend. Then she informed me she lived near the bus station.

Wow! All at once I realized this was an invitation. I was tired, emotionally spent and alone. I was tempted… but the decision was made 25 years before on my wedding day. I made a decision to be faithful to the amazing woman I married. That solid commitment, made in the past, helped me that day. The temptation was real but the decision was already made.

There are important decisions that can be made in advance. In fact, making decisions in advance of difficult circumstances can help you hold to values or commitments. **Preemptive Decision Making is making a decision before you find yourself in a challenging situation.**

ACTION How has this principle been helpful to you in the past? Are there any decisions you have already made that it would be helpful to re-affirm now? Are there some clear, solid preemptive decisions it would be helpful to make now in order to safeguard your relationship in the future?

Problems or Opportunities?

© GETTY IMAGES/THINKSTOCK

39

Years ago I was sitting in a university cafeteria. Behind me I heard someone say, "I don't have problems. I just have opportunities, to trust God!" That statement stuck with me over the years. I have become convinced it is true. Problems can be opportunities, depending on perspective.

Shortly after we were married, the first wave of conflict hit. My wife and I made the commitment to have the attitude that problems would be building blocks not stumbling stones in our relationship.

Every relationship has challenges and difficulties. A positive attitude can make a big difference in the successful navigation through each challenge.

Each problem can be transformed into an opportunity in at least three ways.

- Productively working through difficulties builds strength and depth in your relationship.
- Each managed problem builds a foundation to face the next challenge which will come!
- Trusting that God does indeed love you and has a plan that is good keeps you focused forward to see the revelation of that plan.

ACTION **Check** your attitude when problems come (because they will), and **ask** where is the opportunity in this problem?

Decide this will be a building block to make your relationship better.

Consider your connection with God. How are you doing spiritually? A relationship with God provides an unshakable foundation in difficult moments. **Check out** the Resource section at the end of this book for spiritual insights.

Fighters and Cave Dwellers!

© GETTY IMAGES/TOP PHOTO GROUP/THINKSTOCK

40

There are two extremes in conflict. I call them the **fighters** and the **cave dwellers.** Fighters are up for a good argument at any moment. Two fighters could have a volatile relationship but still learn to function well because they have found a productive way to handle their conflict. They blow up, solve, make up and move on. Not my style but the pattern works for some. The danger can be the cumulative damage of a harsh process that could be hurtful.

Another extreme… Cave dwellers respond to conflict by withdrawing. Two people in a relationship with this tendency will either bury the issue or process it internally. In the best case scenario, the internal processor may decide it is not a big deal and decide to let it go, or come out of the cave to discuss the conflict after time for personal reflection. In the worst case scenario, the person will bury issue after issue. They miss out on productive conflict and the relational growth that could result. Plus there is the danger of deep bitterness that gradually builds to the point that a note on the fridge says, "I'm done!"

ACTION On a scale of 0-10, with 0 being "cave dwellers" and 10 being "fighters," decide where you each are in your relational conflict style. To what degree do issues get identified, discussed, resolved? What one thing could you do to improve your way of dealing with conflict?

Productive conflict happens when issues are identified and solutions are set in motion.

Rekindled

41

M any men have asked me some variation on the question, "My wife wants to give up on our marriage. How do I save our marriage?" Rekindling a relationship at this point is not an "easy fix!" It will take time and patience. Here are some suggestions for both men and women to consider:

- **Take responsibility.** Affirm your love and desire to do whatever it will take. Apologize for any hurts you have caused whether intentionally or unintentionally. State what you plan to do differently to ensure that whatever you did will not happen again.
- **Unpack baggage.** Begin the process of discovering where things have gotten off track. When did things start to go wrong? Was it an event? Was it just a slow drift? Do not be defensive. Make it your goal to get the issues out in the open to begin moving in a positive direction. A third party you both trust or a marriage mentor/counselor might be needed to help you through the process.
- **Woo to Rekindle.** If your partner has lost hope in your relationship, this might be a one-sided plan, at first. Think back to when you first "fell in love"... What did you like doing together? Begin doing those things again. Be intentional about performing daily acts of kindness, saying words of appreciation and focusing positive attention on your spouse. Woo them by rebuilding connections.
- **Don't do it alone.** Seek out another person or couple who can encourage, listen and offer practical suggestions.

SUGGESTED RESOURCE *Rekindled* by Pat and Jill Williams

42

In July 1952, Florence Chadwick waded into the waters off Catalina Island. Her goal was to swim the Channel to the coast of California. The numbing cold of the water hit her; she could barely see the boat that accompanied her in the **dense fog**. Several times during her swim, a rifle was fired to keep sharks away. She swam for 15 hours.

Florence was no stranger to long distance swimming. She had been the first woman to swim the English Channel in both directions. But this day, all she could see was the fog. She was exhausted, and felt discouraged.

Her trainer encouraged her to keep going, but Florence gave up, less than a kilometer from her goal! In the interview after the swim, she was quoted as saying, **"If I had only been able to see the land, I might have been able to make it."** Two months later, she was successful and set a new speed record in the process.

The fog kept Florence Chadwick from her goal. How about you? **"Relational fog"** can be anything that distracts you from your goal of a deep and enduring relationship, things like busyness, exhaustion, discouragement or financial pressures.

ACTION Evaluate together: What "relational fog" is keeping you from an intimate and growing relationship? Evaluate the extent to which busyness, exhaustion, discouragement or financial pressures are creating fog in your relationship. What is one step you can take to "clear the fog"?

43

While there are many factors that shape relationships, commitment is the glue that keeps them together. There are three components of commitment which shape relationships: Emotion, Intellect and Will. None of them can stand on their own.

Positive emotions provide the catalyst necessary for the relationship to begin and continue. Intellect points out the logic of the relationship: we have the same goals in life; we have the same values. The relationship makes sense. Will determines the strength of a relationship as it is the commitment to make it work.

A new relationship seems to depend on feelings at first, whether for good or for bad. "It feels so right to be together!" Or, "The feelings are gone." If feelings are the only glue, the relationship will not last through the storms ahead. If intellect is the only glue, there may be times when staying together may not "make sense." For instance, is it logical to stay with someone who has had an affair? Someone who has Alzheimer's? Simple logic might say no. If will, or pure determination, is the only glue in the relationship then it might seem cold and unfeeling, even if you do stay together.

The three together are powerful. The will holds steady when the feelings are weak. Feelings buoy the relationship and the mind filters complex emotions.

ACTION Consider how have these three factors shaped and developed your relationship? How does that impact your relationship?

King Solomon once reflected…

> "A cord of three strands is not quickly torn apart."

> *– Ecclesiastes 4:12b*

Disappointed?

44

Everyone has some level of disappointment in relationships: not every hope, wish, dream or expectation can be met by one person. When expectations are impossible to fulfill, disappointment can become a crisis. In their book, *Relationships*, Drs. Les and Leslie Parrott state, "Too many people attach themselves to another person to obtain approval, affirmation, purpose, safety and of course, identity. And when the inevitable disappointment happens, they complain bitterly that this person failed them."

Two issues are at stake here. First, it's crucial to have a foundation for your own well-being. It is important to recognize that everyone has deep needs that go beyond what another person can fill. Consider this thought from 17th century philosopher, Blaise Pascal:

> *"There is a God-shaped vacuum in the heart of every man which cannot be filled by any created thing, but only by God, the Creator, made known through Jesus."*

Second, embrace the fact that **all** relationships have disappointments! Perfection only exists in heaven. Working through your disappointments can actually make your relationship better. When you feel disappointed, figure out why and take positive action rather than complain or give up.

ACTION Evaluate: Are you stuck in disappointment? Do your unmet expectations rob you of the good elements of your relationships? How strong are the spiritual foundations in your life? Do you understand how God can give you supernatural resources that will impact every relationship? If you are not sure, check out the Spiritual Resource section at the end of this book.

SUGGESTED RESOURCE *Relationships* by Drs. Les and Leslie Parrott

Schedule Sex?

© GETTY IMAGES/JSTOCKPHOTO/THINKSTOCK

45

S chedule Sex? Sounds crazy! That was my first thought and it may be yours also. Consider some of the possible benefits. With busy schedules and the tiredness that results, having a point of connection scheduled could help take the stress out of the equation and allow for emotional and mental anticipation. It may remove some of the anxiety of deciding in the moment whether or not to initiate or respond.

Some couples have found scheduling sex very energizing. It allows for some creativity that requires preparation, like setting the atmosphere, choosing appealing clothing or any other number of creative touches. Sex in your schedule could also help where conflicting libidos are involved, allowing compromise on frequency of sex. This does not preclude spontaneity but it does provide a base line of sexual enjoyment in over-complicated lives!

We put our priorities into our schedules. The physical expression of love is a powerful bonding agent in any relationship. It is a priority to a healthy and growing relationship.

ACTION Talk about scheduling sex. Set a few dates. Try it for a month or two.

Just in case you're wondering…

> "Adults, on average, have sex about 61 times per year, or slightly more than once a week, according to University of Chicago's National Opinion Research Center. Marital status and age are key influences in sexual activity."
>
> *- Christopher J. Gearon, "Sex in Marriage: Better Sex in Marriage"*

46

In their book, *Rekindling the Romance,* Dennis and Barbara Rainey state that a romantically satisfying relationship has three nonnegotiable elements: Security, Acceptance and Emotional Connection. A good physical, sexual relationship develops from these qualities.

Relational security is characterized by safety. This safety is multifaceted. It can include physical, financial and emotional elements. Feeling safe physically can be as simple as having a good security system. Financial security can be enhanced by consistent communication on budget and goals. Security emotionally is characterized by being in touch with each other's joys, disappointments and desires.

Acceptance is a deep belief that you are fully known by another person and are highly valued in spite of your flaws and imperfections. This acceptance can be affirmed with words like, "I love you. I'm committed to you and to our relationship."

Emotional connection comes with shared experiences, thoughts, desires and aspirations. This connection can be maintained and built through being truly intentional about keeping in touch with the internal world of the other person. My wife asks me questions to find out what is going on inside because I don't naturally talk about feelings and she feels emotionally connected to me when I share honestly and listen to her thoughts/perspective.

ACTION Take an inventory of each of these three areas. Discuss where you are doing well and how you can improve in each.

SUGGESTED RESOURCE *Rekindling the Romance* by Dennis and Barbara Rainey

It's all About Timing

47

When are the best times to talk? Not during the football game or when there are lots of distractions or when you are in a hurry. Generally when a person is hungry, under pressure and/or tired they are not their best for deep, constructive conversation. Timing is especially important when you are dealing with sensitive issues. At night just before bed may not be good but right after dinner might be a better time for significant conversations. Each couple needs to find the "sweet spot" for productive dialogue. My wife has reminded me several times she is not a night person so late at night is not a good time for her to respond to complex issues. Our best time is right after dinner.

Consider timing...! It is okay to say, "This is an important topic. We do need to talk about this but I cannot give it my best now. Can we do it tomorrow after dinner?" Location is important also. If you are concerned about emotions getting the best of the conversation going to a coffee shop might help keep the lid on things. Turn off technology to reduce distractions.

Experiment: If you are having difficulty getting good one on one talk time, maybe agree on 15 minute windows that fits 2 or 3 times into the weekly schedule as a starting point. See which work the best.

Wisdom from Solomon:

"A gentle answer turns away wrath, but a harsh word stirs up anger."

– Proverbs 15:1 NIV

48

How do you put passion back into your relationship? What do you do to fan the flames? Jim Burns in his book, *Creating an Intimate Marriage,* suggests developing a plan to re-ignite those sparks. His suggestions:

- 15 seconds   Passionate kiss every day.
- 15 minutes   Connect 5 times a week to talk.
- 1.5 hours   Date once a week.
- 1.5 hours   Sexual intimacy blocked in the schedule.

Sound simple? Overwhelming? It could be fun. The key is to start where you are in your relationship and build from there. A passionate 15 second kiss that doesn't demand immediate gratification can rekindle some of those "wow" feelings. A big step might be carving out 15 minutes of connection time to talk about your life and reconnect emotionally.

The date can be a simple muffin and coffee in a restaurant or if your budget requires creativity, a candlelight dinner at home. For a period of our lives, breakfast at McDonald's was a date we had each Saturday while our kids were in swimming lessons.

Scheduled sexual intimacy? I schedule many less important activities. I've realized that in the craziness of life this can allow for emotional preparation and keeps sex as a priority in our relationship. Remember this is not a quickie but a slow, pleasure-filled 90 minutes!

ACTION   Talk about the passion level in your relationship. Evaluate separately...on a scale of 0-10, how passionate is your relationship? Share your conclusions and come up with a plan to fan the flame.

SUGGESTED RESOURCE   *Creating an Intimate Marriage* by Jim Burns

49

When my son was about 6 years old, we were visiting friends who had just newly landscaped their yard. As we were taking a tour of their handiwork, my son suddenly grabbed a nearby shrub and pulled it out by the roots. As you can imagine, I was shocked! I soon discovered he had found an earthworm that he was convinced needed a home and to his way of thinking, a good place would be right where that shrub was. Though he was just a little guy, he was easily able to pull out the shrub because it had just been planted. Its root system had not had time to anchor it securely.

Relationships are like that shrub. The roots grow strong through shared experience, communication and even difficulties. That may be why a significant percentage of marriages fail within the first five years. They are easily uprooted. While popular media often communicates a "happy ever after" perspective on relationships, it can foster the sense that building deep roots in marriage is an easy process. So when the first waves of discord come, they are often unexpected and overwhelming.

Growing deep roots also requires relational fertilizer. That includes regularly nurturing your relationship with communication, team work, companionship and shared experiences. And don't forget: developing deep roots also takes time.

ACTION Ask in what way are you intentionally adding fertilizer to your relational soil? Go for walks together. Read an article or book together. Consider a weekend getaway or a conference that will strengthen your relationship.

50

H‌ave you ever thought, "We must be speaking different languages?" Maybe you are right! In the book, *The 5 Love Languages,* Dr. Gary Chapman suggests there are different languages or ways we give and receive love. Use the wrong language and the other person does not get the message!

What language do you speak? What language does your spouse use?

- **Words of Affirmation:** The gift of unsolicited compliments, the reasons behind love.
- **Quality Time:** The gift of full, undivided attention.
- **Receiving Gifts:** The gift selected with thoughtfulness and effort show that you know, care for and value the person.
- **Acts of Service:** The gift of doing anything to ease the burden of responsibilities weighing on your spouse.
- **Physical Touch:** The gift of thoughtful touch like hugs, pats on the back, caresses on the arm or face or holding hands.

Personal Example: My wife feels love when I give her quality time but I like to express love through acts of service. I paint the kitchen to say I love you. While she does appreciate my painting the kitchen, she thinks, "If he loved me we would spend more quality time talking and doing things together."

Question: What love language do you speak? In what way do you like to receive love? In what way do you like to express love? What adjustments need to be made in order to express love effectively to your spouse?

SUGGESTED RESOURCE   *The 5 Love Languages* by Dr. Gary Chapman

51

S igns on our highways warn us of dangers that are ahead. They are placed in strategic locations to alert the un-aware traveler. In the book *The Seven Principles for Making Marriage Work,* Dr. John Gottman discusses four signs that signal a marriage is starting to die.

1. You see your marital problems as severe.
2. Talking things over seems useless so you try to solve problems on your own.
3. You start leading parallel lives.
4. Loneliness sets in.

Are there any warning signs in your relationship? One partner may notice these long before the other, less observant partner. My wife is far more sensitive to the warning signs than I am. I have found it is not wise to ignore her concerns!

ACTION Make a date for coffee in a quiet relaxed coffee shop. Talk with each other, not about the problems in your relationship, but your feelings about your relationship. You could start with:

"I feel overwhelmed and alone right now."

"I feel like we are living parallel lives."

"This makes me feel like our marriage is in danger. How do you feel?"

Work on being honest and on trying to understand each other's feelings. Don't worry about discovering solutions...the fact that you are talking about your feelings will help you reconnect. In this case, the process is a big part of the solution. Have a coffee date once a week to start and see where that goes...

SUGGESTED RESOURCE *The Seven Principles for Making Marriage Work* by Dr. John Gottman

52

In his book, *Creating an Intimate Marriage,* author Jim Burns challenges readers with this idea, "YOU set the mood, tone and atmosphere in your marriage." He also points out you are the ONE person who can make a difference in your marriage. You cannot default to, "If only my spouse would change!"

Are you proactive or reactive? Proactive people take positive steps forward to change the circumstances. Reactive people are shaped by their circumstances.

Are you a thermometer or a thermostat? A thermometer reads the temperature. A thermostat changes the temperature. Make a definite choice this week to be the leader in creating affection, warmth and encouragement.

Experiment: Choose one thing you can do EACH day this week. Ask yourself the following:

- **How can I be more affectionate?** Maybe it's a hug, a kiss or holding hands during the day.
- **How do I communicate warmth?** Maybe it's saying thank you; expressing appreciation for things you take for granted.
- **How can I be more encouraging?** Are you looking at the glass half empty? Tell your spouse one thing you like about him/her each day. Examples: That shirt looks good on you. I like your hair that way. You are a hard worker. You are a good parent. That is a good idea!

DISCUSS Reactive/Proactive and Thermometer/Thermostat: Which are you?

SUGGESTED RESOURCE *Creating an Intimate Marriage,* by Jim Burns

Resource Appendices

BOOK LIST
Close Calls by Dave Carder
Creating an Intimate Marriage by Jim Burns
His Needs, Her Needs by Willard E. Harley Jr.
Intended for Pleasure by Ed Wheat MD
Rekindled by Pat and Jill Williams
Rekindling the Romance, Dennis and Barbara Rainey
Relationships by Drs. Les and Leslie Parrott
The Act of Marriage by Tim and Beverly LaHaye
The Gift of Sex by Clifford and Joyce Penner
The Five Love Languages by Gary Chapman
The 10 Best Decisions a Couple Can Make by Bill and Pam Farrel
The Seven Habits of Highly Effective People by Stephen Covey
The Seven Principles for Making Marriage Work by Dr. John Gottman

DVD SERIES
Marriage Oneness – LifeReady series

WEB RESOURCES
www.familylifecanada.com

QUESTIONS/COMMENTS?
Email: lovethatlasts@familylifecanada.com

Mike's Story

I have concluded that in life you can have lots of activity and material things, but without some foundational relationships, your life ends up being just a lot of empty activities and things. This is a lesson I began to learn a long time ago.

Growing up in rural Michigan, my life could have been described as "the best of times and the worst of times." It was the best of times in that I grew up on a hobby farm that resembled a petting zoo. From time to time we had cats, dogs, pigs, chickens, ducks, sheep, goats, cows and horses. We lived near a river that was great for swimming. Being the youngest of 4, I learned to swim when my older brothers threw me into the deep water and said, "Swim!"

It was the worst of times in that my parents were both alcoholics. When my father drank he would become angry and violent. As a result of the physical violence, my mother ended up in the hospital with a broken bone. Many times they would come home from a night of drinking and fight. Sometimes we would go to the neighbors or just listen in fear from our bedrooms.

One night when I was about 9 years old I remember being called out of bed. My parents told us they were getting a divorce and we needed, right then, to pick the parent with whom we wanted to live. In the midst of this trauma, a cloud of despair moved into my life. I began to think that perhaps life was not worth living.

Around that same time my sister started attending a youth group with a friend at a local church. She started bringing me to Sunday school. I really enjoyed the stories, asked many questions and learned lots.

One day my sister asked me if I had ever invited Christ into my life. I did not understand the question so didn't say much. Later someone else asked a similar question and at the same time explained some simple things about God that helped me understand. They explained that God loved me and had sent His son to die for me. Well, I had always hoped that God loved me. I knew the story about Christ dying on the cross but I had never thought about His death in a personal sense that He died for me. This friend went on to explain that Christ's death was a payment for my sin. I had a keen sense of my own sin! She pointed out that Christ desired to come into my life but I had to open the door and allow Him in. If I did He would come in, forgive my sins, be with me always and give me eternal life. I wanted all that but never understood how it could be mine before that moment. That day through prayer, I asked Christ to come in to my life. I did not hear any voices from heaven and there were no lightning bolts just a deep confidence that Christ had indeed done what I had asked.

In the days that follow I started to see some changes. As I understood more about God's love and forgiveness, I began to be able to love and forgive myself, as well as others around me. An example of this was in my relationship with my father. I had a lot of anger and bitterness toward my dad. Slowly I realized that I was being a hypocrite. How could I not forgive and love my father after personally experiencing God's love and forgiveness? I began to ask God to give me the strength to love and forgive him. The day came when I could tell him that I loved him. It was a very emotional moment for both of us. Through that God transformed our relationship. My father has now passed away. I'm so thankful for the change God created in our relationship and in many other relationships in my life since. Experiencing God's love and forgiveness has given me a new template for understanding and power to live out relationships with people around me.

My life can still be characterized by "the best of times and the worst of times" but the difference is I have a foundational relationship with God that provides a solid basis for a life.

T**he greatest need human beings have is to love and be loved. All of my life, I've wrestled with these needs.**

As a child, I grew up in a stable home environment and for the most part, I was happy. But **I never felt I measured up or merited love.** I'd drive myself to be as perfect as I could be, to get A's in school, to be obedient, and to try to please people so that they'd love me. My desire to please others was strong, but it did not bring me peace or the love that I sought.

In high school, I fell in love with a guy named Mike. I convinced my family to attend his church, I worked in student government with him, and I missed him the summer he went to Switzerland on a student exchange. We even ended up going to the same university. I so desperately wanted him to feel the same love for me, but while we were friends, he was also interested in dating others. I did a lot of crying over this guy. The good news is that I did eventually marry him.

Finally, I had my dream-come-true in marriage…right? In the first two years of our marriage, I realized that Mike didn't just want to sit home with me and spend quality time together. He was a very active, people-oriented guy, who either wanted to go out and socialize or else bring lots of people into our home. I, on the other hand, wanted quiet, romantic evenings together, and I began to question whether he really loved me.

After two years, our son was born, followed by three daughters. I poured my love into our children. I had always loved kids. But these children were a handful 24 hours a day! I tried to be a supermom, but I was disillusioned with motherhood some days, questioning whether they really loved me, and if I was even loveable, especially on the days that I would lose my temper with them.

All I ever wanted was to love my husband and my children and have them return

that love. They gave me what love they had but sometimes it just wasn't enough. I now realize that none of them could meet my need for unconditional love.

Not that I was the greatest source of unconditional love, myself! I had, and still have, a hard time loving people. I acknowledge that I am self-centered and often thinking of my own needs over those of others. I have come to realize that if I want to experience unconditional love, and learn how to love others unconditionally, I have to find this love outside of myself!

I have always believed in God and when I realized He loved me just as I am, I knew I needed that kind of love. He created me, and He has become my Source of unconditional love that lasts for a lifetime!

I also now understand that there is sin in my life. Sin was what wrecked my relationships with others because I was self-centered and I knew it. I wanted to be perfect as a child, but I wasn't able to do it. I needed a way to deal with my self-centeredness, to forgive others for the way they treated me and get on with my life in a positive way.

But what was I to do with this sin I wanted to get rid of? I learned that I need to confess it to God and He'd forgive me and cleanse me inside, based on Jesus' death on the cross. No one else volunteered to give His life so that my sins could be forgiven, except Jesus. This was the freedom from sin and selfishness that I was looking for!

It was my choice. I could accept Jesus as my Savior from sin or I could continue to try doing it on my own. Gratefully taking what God offered me seemed like an offer too good to turn down, and even today, I still make a conscious choice to draw on the love of God, for myself and for blessing others.

I still want love from my husband and kids. But I'm not dependent on them for the

unconditional love I need. Only God can give me that kind of love. And knowing God, the source of real love, frees me to love others.

    Reflect: What about you? Do you feel you are getting all the love you want or need out of your relationships? Do you, like me, desire to experience unconditional love? You can! Simply express your desire to God through prayer. God knows your heart so it doesn't matter which words you use, but here's a suggested prayer:

Lord Jesus, I want to know you personally. Thank you for dying on the cross for my sins. I open the door of my life to you and ask you to come in as my Saviour and Lord. Take control of my life. Thank you for forgiving my sins and giving me eternal life. Make me the kind of woman you want me to be. Help me to find everything I need in you and to be more loving to others.

    Does this prayer express the desire of your heart? You can pray it right now, and Jesus Christ will come into your life, just as He promised.

    If you invited Christ into your life, thank God often that He is in your life, that He will never leave you and that you have eternal life. As you learn more about your relationship with God, and how much He loves you, you'll experience life to the fullest, with enough unconditional love to last for a lifetime!

AUTHOR'S NOTE

On the last few pages Karen and I have given you a small snap shot of our personal faith journey. The next two articles explain in more detail how a personal relationship with God can impact your life and the lives of those around you.

This presentation contains a message of love and hope. An exciting adventure awaits those who discover these life-changing truths.

The following four principles will help you discover how to know God personally and experience the abundant life He promised.

GOD'S PERSPECTIVE

1 God loves you and created you to know Him personally. He has a wonderful plan for your life.

God's Love

> "God so loved the world, that He gave His only begotten Son, that whoever believes in Him should not perish, but have eternal life" (John 3:16).

God's Plan

> "Now this is eternal life: that they may know you, the only true God, and Jesus Christ, whom you have sent" (John 17:3)

What prevents us from knowing God personally?

2 People are sinful and separated from God, so we cannot know Him personally or experience His love and plan.

People are Sinful

"All have sinned and fall short of the glory of God" *(Romans 3:23)*.

People were created to have fellowship with God; but, because of our own stubborn self-will, we chose to go our own independent way and fellowship with God was broken. This self-will, characterized by an attitude of active rebellion or passive indifference, is an evidence of what the Bible calls sin.

People are Separated

"The wages of sin is death" [spiritual separation from God] *(Romans 6:23)*.

This diagram illustrates that God is holy and people are sinful. A great gulf separates the two. The arrows illustrate that people are continually trying to reach God and establish a personal relationship with Him through our own efforts, such as a good life, philosophy, or religion, but we inevitably fail.

The third principle explains the only way to bridge this gulf...

GOD'S RESPONSE

3

Jesus Christ is God's only provision for our sin. Through Him alone we can know God personally and experience God's love and plan.

He Died in Our Place

> "God demonstrates His own love toward us, in that while we were yet sinners, Christ died for us" *(Romans 5:8).*

He Rose From the Dead

> "Christ died for our sins...He was buried...He was raised on the third day according to the Scriptures...He appeared to Peter, then to the twelve. After that He appeared to more than five hundred..." *(1 Corinthians 15:3-6).*

He is the Only Way to God

> "Jesus said to him, 'I am the way, and the truth, and the life; no one comes to the Father, but through Me'" *(John 14:6).*

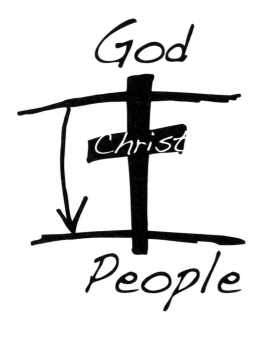

This diagram illustrates that God has bridged the gulf that separates us from Him by sending His Son, Jesus Christ, to die on the cross in our place to pay the penalty for our sins.

It is not enough just to know these truths...

4

We must individually receive Jesus Christ as Savior and Lord; then we can know God personally and experience His love.

We Must Receive Christ

> "As many as received Him, to them He gave the right to become children of God, even to those who believe in His name" *(John 1:12)*

We Receive Christ Through Faith

> "For it is by grace you have been saved, through faith — and this is not from yourselves, it is the gift of God — not by works that no one can boast" *(Ephesians 2:8,9).*

When We Receive Christ, We Experience a New Birth

> *(Read John 3:1-8.)*

We Receive Christ by Personal Invitation

> [Christ speaking] "Here I am! I stand at the door and knock. If any one hears My voice and opens the door, I will come in to him and eat with him and he with Me." *(Revelation 3:20).*

Receiving Christ involves turning to God from self (repentance) and trusting Christ to come into our lives to forgive us of our sins and to make us what He wants us to be. Just to agree intellectually that Jesus Christ is the Son of God and that He died on the cross for our sins is not enough. Nor is it enough to have an emotional experience. We receive Jesus Christ by faith, as an act of our will.

These two circles represent two kinds of lives.

A life without Jesus Christ

Self is in the center and on the throne; Christ (✝) is outside.

A life entrusted to Christ

Christ is in the center and on the throne, and self yields to Christ.

Which circle best describes your life?
Which circle would you like to have represent your life?

The following explains how you can receive Christ...

YOU CAN RECEIVE CHRIST RIGHT NOW BY FAITH THROUGH PRAYER

(Prayer is talking with God)

God knows your heart and is not so concerned with your words as He is with the attitude of your heart. The following is a suggested prayer:

> "Lord Jesus, I want to know You personally. Thank You for dying on the cross for my sins. I open the door of my life and receive You as my Savior and Lord. Thank You for forgiving me of my sins and giving me eternal life. Take control of the throne of my life. Make me the kind of person You want me to be."

Does this prayer express the desire of your heart?

If it does, pray this prayer right now, and Christ will come into your life, as He promised.

HOW TO KNOW THAT CHRIST IS IN YOUR LIFE

Did you receive Christ into your life?

According to His promise in Revelation 3:20, where is Christ right now in relation to you? Christ said that He would come into your life and be your friend so you can know Him personally. Would He mislead you? On what authority do you know that God has answered your prayer? (The trustworthiness of God Himself and His Word.)

The Bible Promises Eternal Life to All Who Receive Christ

> "The witness is this, that God has given us eternal life, and this life is in His Son. He who has the Son has the life; he who does not have the Son of God does not have the life. These things I have written to you who believe in the name of the Son of God, in order that you may know that you have eternal life" *(1 John 5:11-13).*

Thank God often that Christ is in your life and that He will never leave you (Hebrews 13:5). You can know on the basis of His promise that Christ lives in you and that you have eternal life from the very moment you invite Him in. He will not deceive you.

AN IMPORTANT REMINDER...

Do Not Depend on Feelings

The promise of God's Word, the Bible — not our feelings — is our authority. The Christian lives by faith (trust) in the trustworthiness of God Himself and His Word. Flying a jet can illustrate the relationship among fact (God and His Word), faith (our trust in God and His Word), and feeling (The result of our faith and obedience) (John 14:21).

To be transported by a jet, we must place our faith in the trustworthiness of the aircraft and the pilot who flies it. Our feelings of confidence or fear do not affect the ability of the jet to transport us, but they do affect how much we enjoy the trip. In the same way, we as Christians do not depend on feelings or emotions, but we place our faith (trust) in the trustworthiness of God and the promises of His Word.

NOW THAT YOU HAVE RECEIVED CHRIST

The moment that you received Christ by faith, as an act of the will, many things happened, including the following:

- ▸ Christ came into your life (Revelation 3:20 ; Colossians 1:27).

- ▸ Your sins were forgiven (Colossians 1:14).

- ▸ You became a child of God (John 1:12).

- ▸ You received eternal life (John 5:24).

- ▸ You began the great adventure for which God created you (John 10:10; 2 Corinthians 5:17 ; 1 Thessalonians 5:18).

Can you think of anything more wonderful that could happen to you than receiving Christ? Would you like to thank God in prayer right now for what He has done for you? By thanking God, you demonstrate your faith.

To enjoy your new life to the fullest...

SUGGESTIONS FOR CHRISTIAN GROWTH

Spiritual growth results from trusting Jesus Christ. "The righteous man shall live by faith" (Galatians 3:11). A life of faith will enable you to trust God increasingly with every detail of your life, and to practice the following:

G **Go** to God in prayer daily (John 15:7).

R **Read** God's Word daily (Acts 17:11); begin with the Gospel of John.

O **Obey** God moment by moment (John 14:21).

W **Witness** for Christ by your life and words (Matthew 4:19; John 15:8).

T **Trust** God for every detail of your life (1 Peter 5:7).

H **Holy Spirit**—allow Him to control and empower your daily life and witness (Galatians 5:16,17; Acts 1:8).

Remember

Your walk with Christ depends on what you allow Him to do in and through you empowered by the Holy Spirit, not what you do for Him through self effort.

Fellowship in a Good Church

God's Word instructs us not to forsake "the assembling of ourselves together" (Hebrews 10:25). Several logs burn brightly together; but put one aside on the cold hearth and the fire goes out. So it is with your relationship with other Christians.

If you do not belong to a church, do not wait to be invited. Take the initiative; call the pastor of a nearby church where Christ is honored and His Word is preached. Start this week, and make plans to attend regularly.

If you have come to know Christ personally through this presentation of the gospel or would like further help in getting to know Christ better, two sites are recommended:

www.startingwithGod.com or www.LooktoJesus.com

Satisfied?

D o you desire more? Jesus said, "If anyone is thirsty, let him come to me and drink. Whoever believes in me, as the Scripture has said, streams of living water will flow from within him" (John 7:37, 38).

What did Jesus mean? John, the biblical author, went on to explain, "By this he meant the Spirit, whom those who believed in him were later to receive. Up to that time the Spirit had not been given, since Jesus had not yet been glorified" (John 7:39).

Jesus promised that God's Holy Spirit would satisfy the thirst, or deepest longings, of all who believe in Jesus Christ. However, many Christians do not understand the Holy Spirit or how to experience Him in their daily lives.

The following principles will help you understand and enjoy God's Spirit.

The Divine Gift

Divine: (adj.) given by God

God has given us His Spirit so that we can experience intimacy with Him and enjoy all He has for us.

The Holy Spirit is the source of our deepest satisfaction.

The Holy Spirit is God's permanent presence with us.
Jesus said, "I will ask the Father, and he will give you another Counselor to be with you forever—the Spirit of truth" (John 14:16, 17).

The Holy Spirit enables us to understand and experience all God has given us.
"We have not received the spirit of the world but the Spirit who is from God, that we may understand what God has freely given us" (1 Corinthians 2:12).

The Holy Spirit enables us to experience many things:
- A genuine new spiritual life (John 3:1–8).
- The assurance of being a child of God (Romans 8:15, 16).
- The infinite love of God (Romans 5:5; Ephesians 3:18, 19).

Life Without the Spirit | **Life With the Spirit**
Before Receiving Christ | *After Receiving Christ*

Faith

The man without the Spirit does not accept the things that come from the Spirit of God, for they are foolishness to him, and he cannot understand them, because they are spiritually discerned. (1 Corinthians 2:14).

The spiritual man makes judgments about all things…We have the mind of Christ (1 Corinthians 2:15, 16).

But those who are controlled by the Holy Spirit think about things that please the Spirit (Romans 8:5, NLT).

—>Why are many Christians not satisfied in their experience with God?

The Present Danger

Danger: (n.) a thing that may cause injury, loss, or pain

We cannot experience intimacy with God and enjoy all He has for us if we fail to depend on His Spirit.

People who trust in their own efforts and strength to live the Christian life will experience failure and frustration, as will those who live to please themselves rather than God.

We cannot live the Christian life in our own strength.

"Are you so foolish? After beginning with the Spirit, are you now trying to attain your goal by human effort?" (Galatians 3:3).

We cannot enjoy all God desires for us if we live by our self-centered desires.

"For the sinful nature desires what is contrary to the Spirit, and the Spirit what is contrary to the sinful nature. They are in conflict with each other, so that you do not do what you want" (Galatians 5:17).

Three Kinds of Lifestyles

A Self-centered Life	A Christ-centered Life	A Self-centered Life
Before Receiving Christ	*After Receiving Christ*	

"Brothers, I could not address you as spiritual, but as worldly—mere infants in Christ. I gave you milk, not solid food, for you were not yet ready for it. Indeed, you are still not ready. You are still worldly. For since there is jealousy and quarreling among you, are you not worldly? Are you not acting like mere men?" (1 Corinthians 3:1–3).

—>**How can we develop a lifestyle of depending on the Spirit?**

The Intimate Journey

Journey: (n.) any course from one experience to another

By walking in the Spirit we increasingly experience intimacy with God and enjoy all He has for us.

Walking in the Spirit moment by moment is a lifestyle. It is learning to depend upon the Holy Spirit for His abundant resources as a way of life.

As we walk in the Spirit, we have the ability to live a life pleasing to God.
"So I say, live by the Spirit, and you will not gratify the desires of the sinful nature…Since we live by the Spirit, let us keep in step with the Spirit" (Galatians 5:16, 25).

As we walk in the Spirit, we experience intimacy with God and all He has for us.
"But the fruit of the Spirit is love, joy, peace, patience, kindness, goodness, faithfulness, gentleness and self-control" (Galatians 5:22, 23).

The Christ-centered Life

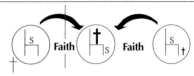

Faith (trust in God and His promises) is the only way a Christian can live by the Spirit.

Spiritual breathing is a powerful word picture which can help you experience moment-by-moment dependence upon the Spirit.

Exhale: Confess your sin the moment you become aware of it—agree with God concerning it and thank Him for His forgiveness, according to 1 John 1:9 and Hebrews 10:1–25. Confession requires repentance—a change in attitude and action.

Inhale: Surrender control of your life to Christ, and rely upon the Holy Spirit to fill you with His presence and power by faith, according to His **command** (Ephesians 5:18) and **promise** (1 John 5:14, 15).

—>How does the Holy Spirit fill us with His power?

The Empowering Presence

Empower: (v.) to give ability to

We are filled with the Spirit by faith, enabling us to experience intimacy with God and enjoy all He has for us.

The essence of the Christian life is what God does in and through us, not what we do for God. Christ's life is reproduced in the believer by the power of the Holy Spirit. To be filled with the Spirit is to be directed and empowered by Him.

By faith, we experience God's power through the Holy Spirit.

"I pray that out of his glorious riches he may strengthen you with power through his Spirit in your inner being, so that Christ may dwell in your hearts through faith" (Ephesians 3:16, 17).

Three important questions to ask yourself:

1. Am I ready now to surrender control of my life to our Lord Jesus Christ? (Romans 12:1, 2)

2. Am I ready now to confess my sins? (1 John 1:9) Sin grieves God's Spirit (Ephesians 4:30). But God in His love has forgiven all of your sins—past, present, and future—because Christ has died for you.

3. Do I sincerely desire to be directed and empowered by the Holy Spirit? (John 7:37–39)

By faith claim the fullness of the Spirit according to His command and promise:

God COMMANDS us to be filled with the Spirit.

"…be filled with the Spirit" (Ephesians 5:18).

God PROMISES He will always answer when we pray according to His will.

"This is the confidence we have in approaching God: that if we ask anything according to his will, he hears us. And if we know that he hears us—whatever we ask—we know that we have what we asked of him" (1 John 5:14, 15).

—>*How to pray to be filled with the Holy Spirit…*

The Turning Point

Turning point: time when a decisive change occurs

We are filled with the Holy Spirit by faith alone.

Sincere prayer is one way of expressing our faith. The following is a suggested prayer:

> Dear Father, I need You. I acknowledge that I have sinned against You by directing my own life. I thank You that You have forgiven my sins through Christ's death on the cross for me. I now invite Christ to again take His place on the throne of my life. Fill me with the Holy Spirit as You commanded me to be filled, and as You promised in Your Word that You would do if I asked in faith. I pray this in the name of Jesus. I now thank You for filling me with the Holy Spirit and directing my life.

Does this prayer express the desire of your heart? If so, you can pray right now and trust God to fill you with His Holy Spirit.

How to know that you are filled by the Holy Spirit

- Did you ask God to fill you with the Holy Spirit?
- Do you know that you are now filled with the Holy Spirit?
- On what authority? (On the trustworthiness of God Himself and His Word: Hebrews 11:6; Romans 14:22, 23.)

As you continue to depend on God's Spirit moment by moment you will experience and enjoy intimacy with God and all He has for you—a truly rich and satisfying life.

An important reminder…
Do Not Depend on Feelings

The promise of God's Word, the Bible—not our feelings—is our authority. The Christian lives by faith (trust) in the trustworthiness of God Himself and His Word. Flying in an airplane can illustrate the relationship among fact (God and His Word), faith (our trust in God and His Word), and feeling (the result of our faith and obedience) (John 14:21).

To be transported by an airplane, we must place our faith in the trustworthiness of the aircraft and the pilot who flies it. Our feelings of confidence or fear do not affect the ability of the airplane to transport us, though they do affect how much we enjoy the trip. In the same way, we as Christians do not depend on feelings or emotions, but we place our faith (trust) in the trustworthiness of God and the promises of His Word.

Now That You are Filled with the Holy Spirit

Thank God that the Spirit will enable you:

- To glorify Christ with your life (John 16:14).
- To grow in your understanding of God and His Word (1 Corinthians 2:14, 15).
- To live a life pleasing to God (Galatians 5:16–23).

Remember the promise of Jesus:
"But you will receive power when the Holy Spirit comes on you; and you will be my witnesses in Jerusalem, and in all Judea and Samaria, and to the ends of the earth" *(Acts 1:8).*

Adapted from Have You Made the Wonderful Discovery of the Spirit-filled Life? written by Bill Bright, © 1966. Published by Campus Crusade for Christ, 375 Hwy 74 South, Suite A, Peachtree City, GA 30269. www.campuscrusade.org

Acknowledgements

Seldom in life is anything produced by one person's actions alone! This book is no exception. Hours have been invested by several people to see this project completed. Thank you to:

Beth Scholes, Sylvia Thompson, Tiffany Goertzen and **Roger Melnychuk** who helped shape this book through their patience, wisdom, suggestions and hours of editing.

Bill Glasgow who moved an idea to reality with care, attention to detail and layout design that was both meticulous and masterful!

Karen Woodard who discussed ideas, was my first line of review in the process and has walked with me for 34 years of marriage. Many of these insights were learned because of her patience, wisdom and forgiveness through the highs and lows of our life together.

Notes